Contents

Introduction

Warming the Earth 4

Is the Earth really getting hotter? 6

Some places are hotter than others 8

Measuring global temperature 10

Causes of global warming

The carbon cycle 12

What are the greenhouse gases? 14

Natural sources of greenhouse gases 16

Human causes of greenhouse gases 18

Effects on plants and ecosystems

What could global warming do? 20

CASE STUDY Bleaching the Great Barrier Reef 22

Plants and the warming planet 24

CASE STUDY The Sundarbans 26

Effects on animals and people

Animals and the warming planet 28

CASE STUDY The Rocky Mountains 30

Living on a warming planet 32

CASE STUDY Florida, the Sunshine State 34

Protection and conservation

World leaders meet 36

Fighting water 38

Storing carbon 40

What happens next?

New methods, new devices 42

What can I do? 44

Glossary 46

Finding out more 47

Index 48

Words that appear in the glossary are printed in bold, **like this**, the first time they occur in the text.

Warming the Earth

Most of the Earth's heat comes from the Sun. The rest is geothermal heat from hot rocks inside the Earth. Light and heat energy from the Sun travels through space to the planets of the solar system. When the energy reaches the Earth the ground absorbs it. Then the ground surface **radiates** the energy back to space as heat. There is a delicate balance between the amount of energy reaching the Earth's surface and the amount of heat being radiated back into space. This balance is what makes our planet the only one in the solar system that can support life.

Screening the Sun

Around the Earth is a layer of gases known as the atmosphere. These gases include oxygen, carbon dioxide, nitrogen, methane and **ozone**. The atmosphere also contains water vapour, tiny specks of dust and haze, as well as clouds. Clouds play an important role in screening the Sun's light energy by reflecting some of this energy back to space. The surfaces of the polar ice caps and deserts are also highly reflective. Together with clouds, they reflect roughly 30 per cent of the Sun's energy back to space. The remaining energy that reaches the Earth's surface warms the ground and the oceans.

Bright clouds over the Earth. Clouds cover an average of 40 per cent of the Earth at any given time.

Fog over Sydney, Australia. Fog is a layer of minute water droplets or ice crystals near the surface of the Earth. Fog reduces visibility for vehicle drivers.

A blanket of gas

Some of the gases in the atmosphere, such as carbon dioxide, methane and ozone, behave like glass in a greenhouse. These gases are called **greenhouse gases**. They let light and heat energy pass through the atmosphere but they trap some of the heat that is radiated back and stop it from leaving the Earth's atmosphere. This keeps our planet comfortably warm at 15 °C (59 °F). Without greenhouse gases, the temperature of our planet would be around –18 °C (0.4 °F), which is too cold for most life. This phenomenon is called the **greenhouse effect**.

Discovering greenhouse gases

The greenhouse effect was first noted in 1827 by Jean Baptiste Fourier, a French **mathematician** and scientist. He suggested that without greenhouse gases, all the heat would escape back into space and the Earth would be about 15 °C (27 °F) colder. In 1859, an Irish scientist named John Tyndall discovered that atmospheric gases could absorb and radiate heat. He conducted experiments that showed that the gases ozone, water vapour and carbon dioxide were the best heat absorbers. In 1896, Swedish scientist Svante Arrhenius suggested that changes in the amount of carbon dioxide in the atmosphere could cause the Earth's temperature to change.

How does a greenhouse work?

The glass in a greenhouse lets in light energy from the Sun. In the greenhouse, the light energy is converted into heat energy, warming the air inside. Heat energy cannot pass through glass well and is trapped in the greenhouse. Our atmosphere behaves like the walls of the greenhouse. It lets in sunlight from space but traps heat and prevents it from returning to space. The greenhouse effect is stronger on some planets and weaker on others. On Venus, for example, the greenhouse effect is so strong that the surface temperature can reach 482 °C (900 °F).

Is the Earth really getting hotter?

The average global temperature today is approximately 15 °C (59 °F). But the Earth's climate has changed over time. The planet's greenhouse effect was strongest between 180 and 30 million years ago. Places like Canada that have a cold climate today were once as warm as Hawaii. Palm trees grew in the Arctic Circle, Antarctica and southern Australia. The Earth began to cool down 30 million years ago when permanent ice caps first formed in eastern Antarctica.

History of the Earth's climate change

The last 2 million years has seen more climate changes than any other time in the Earth's history. This period is known as the Quaternary period. More than nine separate cold and warm spells occurred in the Quaternary period. During the cold spells, known as ice ages, most of the Earth's surface was covered with ice. In between these ice ages there were warm periods known as interstadials. North America experienced its last ice age 70,000 years ago, when 97 per cent of present-day Canada was covered with ice. Global temperatures were lowest 18,000 years ago. The last ice age ended 10,000 years ago and the interstadial known as the Holocene began. This is the period in which we are living now.

Cape Hallet, Antartica, in the South Pole. In summer, more solar radiation reaches the surface of the South Pole than at the equator.

Recent warming

Scientists have found that the Earth's temperature increased by up to 0.6 °C (1 °F) during the 20th century. They believe that one of the main causes of this global warming is the increase in greenhouse gases in the atmosphere. They estimate that if the amount of greenhouse gases continues to increase, the Earth's temperature will continue to rise too, perhaps by up to 3.5° C (6.3 °F) over the coming decades.

Smoke from factories pollutes the air with harmful gases, which trap heat in the atmosphere.

Carbon dioxide on the rise

In the mid-1700s, people began to invent machines to help them do work. This was the start of the period we call the **Industrial Revolution**. Like vehicles today, these machines burned **fossil fuels** for energy, which released greenhouse gases into the atmosphere. More and more machines were built and used. In less than 200 years, the amount of carbon dioxide in the atmosphere increased from 280 parts per million to 360 parts per million. This means that if we divided a sample of air into a million parts, 360 of those parts would be carbon dioxide.

The Geological Time Scale

Our Earth is very old. Its **geological** age is thought to be nearly 4.6 billion years. Each era in the Geological Time Scale is characterized by different conditions and unique **ecosystems**. For instance, dinosaurs lived during the Mesozoic Era, also known as the Age of Reptiles. The Cenozoic Era was when the first ancestors of dogs, cats, horses and monkeys appeared. This era is sometimes called the Age of Mammals.

		The Geological Time Scale		
Eon	**Era**	**Period**		**When began (millions of years before present time)**
Phanerozoic	Cenozoic	Quaternary	Holocene	0.01
			Pleistocene	1.8
		Tertiary	Pliocene	5
			Miocene	23
			Oligocene	34
			Eocene	57
			Paleocene	65
	Mesozoic	Cretaceous		144
		Jurassic		208
		Triassic		245
	Paleozoic	Permian		286
		Carboniferous		360
		Devonian		408
		Silurian		438
		Ordovician		505
		Cambrian		544
Precambrian	Proterozoic			2500
	Archaean			3800
	Hadean			4600

Some places are hotter than others

The coldest place on the Earth is Vostok in Antarctica, where temperatures can reach a low of −89 °C (−128 °F). Some scientists believe that the hottest place on the Earth is Death Valley in California, the USA. Daytime temperatures there reached a high of 57 °C (134 °F) in 1913.

View of Death Valley from Zabriskie Point in California.

Urban heat island effect

Scientists have found that urban areas are 1 to 5.5 °C (1.8 to 10 °F) hotter than the countryside. This is called the 'urban heat island effect'. City roads and buildings are mostly made of concrete and **asphalt**, which are good energy absorbers. The surfaces of roads and buildings absorb light energy during the day and radiate it as heat energy at night. Warm air is less dense than cold air. The warm city air rises and cool air from the surrounding countryside rushes in to take its place. As the warm air rises, it cools down. When this happens, water vapour in the air condenses into water droplets. The droplets join until they become so big that they start to fall as rain. Because of the urban heat island effect, early-morning showers and thunderstorms are common in cities.

Rainstorm in Atlanta, USA, capital of the southern state of Georgia.

Hotspots

Scientists discovered that North America, Europe, Asia and Australia had the highest rate of warming during the 20th century. These places experienced temperature rises of between 0.5 and 0.6 °C (0.8 and 1 °F) from 1950 to 1999. Industrial activity in these parts of the world is high. Oil refineries and factories that burn fossil fuels for making electricity produce air **pollutants**, such as sulphur dioxide and carbon dioxide. As carbon dioxide is a greenhouse gas, it traps heat and warms the Earth's surface.

*An industrial plant releasing smoke and steam into the atmosphere. In 2001, the UK released around 570 **megatonnes** of carbon dioxide into the atmosphere.*

How hot has our Earth become?

Scientists compared temperature readings in the past 1000 years with those taken in the period 1961 to 1990. They found that up until the 1900s, the northern **hemisphere** was cooler than it is today. Then temperatures suddenly started to rise. This was probably the result of increased burning of fossil fuels since the start of the Industrial Revolution.

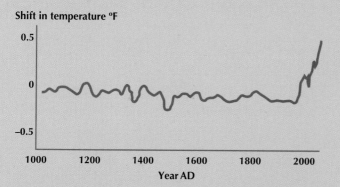

The graph shows roughly 1000 years of temperature change in the northern hemisphere. It is based on combined data taken from tree rings, ice layers and other sources.

Warming the Earth with charcoal

Charcoal is a black substance that is used to cook food on outdoor barbecues. It is made by burning wood in ovens that have little or no air. Charcoal consists mainly of carbon. When it is burned, this carbon is released. On average, about 27 per cent of the carbon in charcoal returns to the atmosphere locked in carbon dioxide molecules. Burning charcoal also releases nitrous oxide, another greenhouse gas.

Measuring global temperature

In 1938, British **meteorologist** Guy Stewart Callendar made the first proper measurement of global temperature. He gathered data from weather stations worldwide and found that the average temperature of the Earth had increased between 1880 and 1930. Sadly, no one took his findings seriously. In 1957, two scientists set up instruments on the Mauna Kea volcano in Hawaii to measure the level of carbon dioxide in the atmosphere. Its records show that the level of carbon dioxide has been increasing steadily since that time and that the Earth is slowly warming up.

Satellites

Satellites are the most efficient and accurate way of measuring climate change. Weather satellites are sent into orbit by rockets or on board space shuttles. As they orbit the Earth, satellites measure the planet's atmosphere using instruments mounted on them. These instruments include heat-sensitive cameras. With these cameras, the satellites can take a picture of a certain area that shows its temperature. The satellite then sends the information back to a control station on the Earth.

A weather observation station. There are more than 3500 weather stations around the world. They take measurements of rainfall, temperature and other conditions.

Weather balloons

Another way of understanding the Earth's climate is to send balloons high up into the atmosphere. Each balloon is fitted with radio transmitters, thermometers and other instruments that measure air temperature, pressure and **humidity**. Meteorologists fill the balloon with helium, a gas that is lighter than air, which causes the balloon to rise. The instruments attached to the balloon record weather information as the balloon rises, or when it reaches a certain altitude. The information is sent to weather stations by the radio transmitters. The balloon finally bursts at an altitude of around 27,400 metres. The instruments are returned to the Earth by a small parachute.

Launch of a weather balloon. About two balloons are launched every day from observation stations around the world.

Fossil evidence

Pollen in fossils provides important clues to **prehistoric** global climates. Pollen falls from trees and plants into the soil and can be preserved for thousands of years. Each plant species produces a unique pollen type. By identifying the type of pollen found in a place, scientists can tell which trees grew there. In tropical regions like Indonesia, scientists have found pollen from plants, such as pine, that can grow in temperate climates. This means that the temperature in the world's tropical areas may have been lower in the past, allowing temperate plants to grow there.

Tree rings

Scientists also study tree rings to learn about the Earth's climate in the past. Trees grow faster in warmer climates than in cooler environments. Each year, the trunk of a tree grows wider. If you chop a tree down, you will see rings in the **cross-section** of the trunk. A tree produces a new ring each year. Scientists measure the width of individual rings to estimate climate conditions at the time each ring was formed. Tree rings grown during warmer years are thicker than those produced in colder years. In this way, scientists can calculate which were the warmer and colder years.

The carbon cycle

Carbon is found in all living things – plants, animals and humans – and nearly everywhere on the Earth. It is found in the atmosphere in the gas carbon dioxide, and dissolved in water in oceans and lakes. It is also found in soil, fossil fuels stored deep in the ground, certain types of rocks and in the shells of animals.

The carbon cycle is a complex cycle that circulates carbon between plants, animals and soil. The exchange of carbon between living and non-living things is very closely balanced. About 100 **gigatonnes** of carbon is captured by plants and oceans each year and about the same amount is released back into the environment. But this natural balance is disturbed by human activities such as burning fossil fuels and **deforestation**. Burning fossil fuels releases more carbon dioxide into the air. Deforestation, on the other hand, results in less carbon dioxide being removed from the atmosphere.

Absorbing carbon dioxide

During the day, green plants absorb carbon dioxide in the air (or dissolved in water) to make food. A green pigment, chlorophyll, helps plants combine carbon dioxide and water to form sugar, using energy from the Sun. As a result of this action, oxygen is given off. This process is known as **photosynthesis**. Through photosynthesis, trees change carbon into wood and they grow bigger and taller. They produce leaves, which absorb even more carbon dioxide. Plants remove about 60 billion tonnes of carbon from the atmosphere each year. Plant-eating animals, such as rabbits, use the carbon in the plants to build their own tissues. Other animals that feed on the rabbits then use the carbon in the rabbits for their own needs.

Forests play a very important role in the carbon cycle. In old forests, huge amounts of carbon are stored in the tree trunks, branches and deep in the soil.

Releasing carbon dioxide

Animals release carbon dioxide into the air each time they breathe out. Carbon dioxide is also released by plants and trees when they **respire**. When animals and plants die, fungi, termites and other small creatures break them down into simpler substances. This process is called **decomposition**. Decomposition returns the carbon in the dead animal or plant into the soil and to the atmosphere as carbon dioxide. Over time, some of the carbon in the soil is transformed into fossil fuels.

Left: Bracket fungi growing on a tree stump. They are so-called because they grow from the side of trees like shelves. Bracket fungi play an important role in decomposing fallen trees, tree stumps and branches.

Watery storehouses

Oceans and green plants are known as carbon sinks. This means that they remove carbon from the atmosphere and store it. Oceans and seas store more than 50 per cent of the Earth's greenhouse gases. When carbon dioxide dissolves in the oceans, it reacts with other chemicals to form new substances, or compounds. For example, carbon dioxide reacts with calcium to form calcium carbonate, a white chalky material. Calcium carbonate is the main compound found in limestone, pearls, coral reefs and clamshells.

The white cliffs of Dover in the UK are calcium carbonate made from millions of fossilized sea creatures and corals.

Eating carbon

Every living thing is a storehouse of carbon. When a caterpillar munches on a leaf, carbon is transferred from the leaf to the caterpillar. The caterpillar uses this carbon to grow bigger before it changes into a butterfly. In the same way, we add carbon into our bodies each time we eat something containing it.

What are the greenhouse gases?

The term greenhouse gas refers to any atmospheric gas that absorbs heat. There are several different greenhouse gases. These include water vapour, carbon dioxide, methane, nitrous oxide and ozone.

Carbon dioxide

Carbon dioxide (CO_2) is a colourless, odourless and **soluble** gas. Carbon dioxide forms about 0.03 per cent of the total gases in the atmosphere. It is made up of one **atom** of carbon and two atoms of oxygen. Carbon dioxide is produced when any living thing respires. The air we exhale is mostly carbon dioxide. Every person exhales about 1.25 litres (0.3 gallons) of carbon dioxide every day.

Methane

Methane (CH_4) is an invisible gas that has no smell. It is made up of carbon and hydrogen. The gas is highly flammable, which means it catches fire easily. The will-o'-the-wisp mentioned in stories is the pale blue flame sometimes seen burning over marshlands. This is actually methane burning.

After carbon dioxide, methane is the second most important greenhouse gas. Scientists believe that methane may have caused up to 20 per cent of the global warming in the last 200 years. Luckily, methane remains in the atmosphere for only twelve years. This means that methane released in the atmosphere today will break down and disappear in the next twelve years. This is brief compared with the amount of time atmospheric carbon dioxide takes to disappear – up to 200 years!

*Angus cattle in the Scottish highlands. Cattle have **bacteria** in their gut that break down food. While doing so, the bacteria release methane gas. A cow can belch up to 0.2 kilograms of methane gas a day.*

Nitrous oxide

Nitrous oxide (N_2O) is a colourless gas with a sweet taste. A molecule of nitrous oxide is formed when two atoms of nitrogen and one atom of oxygen combine. This gas is also known as laughing gas.

In 1800, the English scientist Humphry Davy was the first to discover that the gas could be used as a painkiller. Until the late 1950s, people could buy a minute's worth of nitrous oxide at carnivals, where they would laugh themselves silly after inhaling the gas.

Humphry Davy, who discovered the painkilling effect of nitrous oxide.

Ozone – a good or a bad gas?

Ozone (O_3) is made up of three atoms of oxygen. It is concentrated in the stratosphere, a layer of the atmosphere that lies 9.6 to 50 kilometres (6 to 31 miles) above the Earth's surface. Ozone in the stratosphere acts as a shield that protects the Earth against harmful **ultraviolet** (UV) rays from the Sun. Too much UV radiation will burn our skin and may even cause skin cancer and cataracts in the eyes. But ozone acts as a greenhouse gas where it lies closer to the Earth. And at ground level, ozone is a dangerous pollutant.

Sunbathers need to protect themselves from harmful UV rays by using sunblock.

How much more heat?

Carbon dioxide is the main greenhouse gas in the atmosphere. There is 180 times more carbon dioxide in the air than all the other greenhouse gases, and the amount is increasing. But methane and nitrous oxide absorb more heat than carbon dioxide. One molecule of methane absorbs 21 times more heat than a carbon dioxide molecule. A molecule of nitrous oxide absorbs 310 times more heat than a molecule of carbon dioxide.

Natural sources of greenhouse gases

Some greenhouse gases are released into the atmosphere naturally. Without the natural greenhouse effect, the Earth's global temperature would be at a low of around −18 °C (0.4 °F) instead of the comfortable 15 °C (59 °F) that it is today.

Carbon dioxide

Plant life on the Earth produces about 50 gigatonnes of carbon dioxide a year. In comparison, human beings together produce about 6 gigatonnes of carbon dioxide a year. The oceans produce about 90 gigatonnes of carbon dioxide, which is 50 per cent of all the carbon dioxide released into the atmosphere. Carbon dioxide is stored in the deep ocean waters. Dead fish and plants sink to the ocean floor. They decompose, giving off carbon dioxide in the process. On and near the ocean surface, photosynthesizing plants and organisms like **plankton** remove carbon dioxide from the water.

Scientists estimate that the parts of the Pacific Ocean close to the equator release three-quarters of all the carbon dioxide from oceans. Strong winds blowing across the eastern Pacific Ocean remove heat from the ocean surface. Cold water, which is rich in carbon dioxide, rushes up from the ocean floor to take the place of the warm water. Carbon dioxide is then released into the atmosphere.

Seaweed floating on an ocean surface.

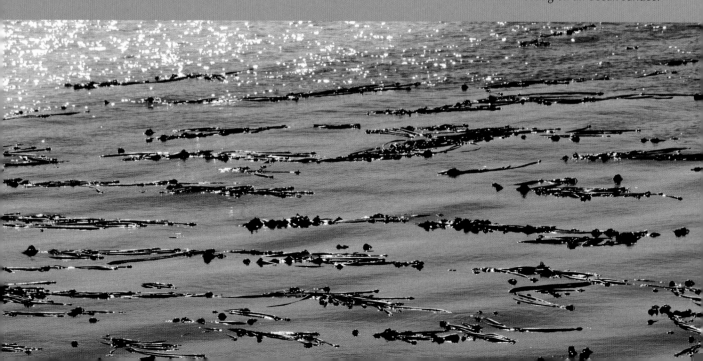

Methane

Each year, about 155 megatonnes of methane are released by natural sources. Wetlands and marshes release about 115 megatonnes of methane every year. The oceans produce another 10 megatonnes of methane yearly.

Did you know that termites produce 20 megatonnes of methane a year? There are two kinds of bacteria living in a termite's gut. When the termite digests wood, a group known as fermentative bacteria help to break down the wood. Another group of bacteria, known as methanogenic bacteria, use waste hydrogen, carbon dioxide and stomach acids as sources of energy. They generate their own waste product, which is methane. The termites release methane from their intestines.

Termites in action. There are about 2000 species of termite. Australia has around 250 species while North America is home to about 40 species.

Floor of a tropical rainforest.

Nitrous oxide

A total of 4 megatonnes of nitrous oxide come from the action of soil bacteria. Wet forest soils produce 3 megatonnes of nitrous oxide each year. The remaining 1 megatonne is released in **savanna** grasslands. Most of the nitrous oxide from soils is made by the interaction of soil bacteria and nitrogen compounds. Nitrous oxide is created when soil bacteria reacts with ammonia in dry soils. In wet soils, soil bacteria converts nitrates to nitrogen, releasing nitrous oxide in the process. Nitrous oxide is also produced during lightning storms. The intense heat and energy in a bolt of lightning is powerful enough to join oxygen and nitrogen molecules in the air, forming nitrous oxide.

Are oceans carbon sinks or sources?

That depends on their temperature. Oceans start to release carbon dioxide when the temperature rises. When the temperature is higher, there is more heat energy in the water. Molecules in the water have more energy to move around. They bump into one another, throwing some carbon dioxide molecules out of the water. As a result, the amount of carbon dioxide dissolved in the water decreases.

Human causes of greenhouse gases

There are over 6 billion people living on the Earth now. Scientists believe this number could increase to 9 billion by 2050. This means that people will clear more forests, set up more farms, drive more motor vehicles and build more industries. Together, these activities will increase global warming and raise the Earth's temperature even further.

Tropical hardwood logging in Sarawak, Southeast Asia.

Deforestation

As the human population increases, forests are cleared for land and to provide firewood and timber to build houses. Today, almost all of the forests in Europe and North America have been cleared. The forests that remain are mostly in tropical areas like the Amazon region of Brazil and Southeast Asia. These forests are disappearing at an alarming rate. Data obtained from satellites show that the rate of destruction in these places has increased to between 64,000 square kilometres (24,710 square miles) and 204,000 square kilometres (78,764 square miles) annually. Scientists estimate that by 2030, 80 per cent of the world's forest will be lost forever. As wood decomposes or is burned for fuel, the carbon stored in trees goes back into the atmosphere as carbon dioxide. According to scientists, deforestation accounts for about 20 per cent of the increase in the release of human-related carbon dioxide since the beginning of the Industrial Revolution.

Agriculture

The soil in many temperate countries lacks nitrogen. Farmers add fertilizers that are rich in nitrogen to the soil to help crops grow. These fertilizers release nitrous oxide. Each year, fertilizers release about 0.3 to 3 megatonnes of nitrous oxide into the atmosphere.

Besides growing crops, we also rear animals for food. Like termites, cattle and sheep have bacteria in their gut that break down food and release methane gas. Today, there are about 1.3 billion cattle in the world. These cattle alone account for 0.3 megatonnes of methane a year.

Right: A small plane sprays fertilizer on a chick-pea crop in Israel.
Below: There are about 600 million motor vehicles in the world today. This number is expected to double in the next 30 years.

Burning fossil fuels

Burning coal for making electricity is the greatest source of man-made greenhouse gases. Another source is petrol, which is the main fuel for motor vehicles. It is a mixture of hydrogen and carbon compounds and **petroleum**. When petrol is burned, the carbon in it combines with oxygen to form carbon dioxide. Burning about 4 litres of petrol gives off 10 kilograms of carbon dioxide along with other greenhouse gases such as nitrous oxide.

Industrialization

Industries produce greenhouse gases including carbon dioxide, nitrous oxide and methane. Scientists estimate that industries emit about 5.4 gigatonnes of carbon dioxide every year. The USA is the largest greenhouse gas producer in the world. Since 1950, industries in the USA have emitted 51 billion tonnes of carbon dioxide. That is roughly one-quarter of the total carbon dioxide produced worldwide. In addition, industries that use coal, natural gas and petroleum release about 100 megatonnes of methane worldwide each year.

Planting rice

Rice is the most important crop in the world. Rice feeds about one-third of the people living on the Earth. More than half of the world's rice is grown in India and China. Most rice is planted in fields flooded with water. Bacteria living in the **waterlogged** soil release up to 60 megatonnes of methane a year.

What could global warming do?

Why are scientists so concerned about the increase in greenhouse gases? What will global warming do to the Earth? Predicting climate change is a very difficult process. Even with the most powerful computers helping us, we cannot be sure what will happen on a warmer planet. We do know that changes in temperature will affect our weather. For example, most climate **models** generated by computers predict the heat will bring violent weather and increased flooding, due to the melting of **glaciers** and polar ice. This will affect all life on the planet, including people.

This tree in Taipei, Taiwan, was uprooted by typhoon Herb on 31 July 1996. The winds blew at up to 234 kilometres (145 miles) per hour.

More violent storms

Global warming could bring about more violent storms. The strength of winds depends on the difference in temperatures over land and sea. As warm air rises, cold air rushes in to take its place. The greater the temperature difference, the stronger the winds are. If the temperature of the Earth's atmosphere rises, then there will be a greater difference between air temperature and ocean temperature. These strong winds create bigger and more violent storms. In 1999, Hurricane Floyd brought floods and strong winds to the east coast of the USA. The storm killed 51 people and left thousands of people homeless.

Ecosystems on a warmer planet

An ecosystem is a community of plants and animals within a physical environment or **habitat**. Any changes to the environment will affect the plants and animals living there. Global warming could bring huge environmental changes. Some animals, such as cockroaches which eat many things, may be able to adapt to these changes. Others will be forced to move in order to survive. In Europe, the sooty copper butterfly was forced to **migrate** from Austria to Estonia because its environment in Austria had become too warm.

Plants and organisms that are physically fixed to their habitats may die. The organisms that create coral reefs, for example, are very sensitive to the temperature of the water they live in. They cannot survive in a temperature below 25 °C (77 °F) or above 29 °C (84.2 °F).

Sea anemone in its habitat. Anemones are sea animals that usually remain fixed to a rock. They use their tentacles to catch food.

Hot spells

Scientists who study the climate are called climatologists. They are worried that an increase in greenhouse gases will cause changes in the Earth's climate. They believe these changes may be happening already. The year 1998 was one of the hottest years ever recorded. In that year, people living in Texas, USA, experienced a hot spell of 38 °C (100.4 °F) for 29 days. Crops withered in the dry weather and many farmers did not have anything to sell. In the same year, India experienced temperatures of 50.6 °C (123 °F), its hottest in 50 years. This **heat wave** killed more than 2500 people.

People cool themselves during a heat wave in London. On 7 August 2003, temperatures in London peaked at 35.9 °C (96.6 °F), making it one of the hottest days of the year.

Glaciers and ice caps

Melting ice is another danger in a warming planet. Ice is found on the Earth as ice caps at the poles. Ice is also found in glaciers on high mountains and in very cold places. Glaciers move very slowly, sometimes only a few centimetres a year. A warmer climate will cause the ice to melt. The water from melting glaciers and the Antarctic ice cap will flow into the oceans and sea levels will rise.

Bleaching the Great Barrier Reef

Coral reefs have survived on the Earth for millions of years. They cover less than 1 per cent of the Earth's surface, yet 50 per cent of the world's marine species live in them. Scientists believe that the reefs contain more than 4000 fish species and 700 types of coral. It is no wonder that scientists describe coral reefs as the 'rainforests of the sea'.

Coral reefs thrive in warm tropical seas. They are mostly found in the Caribbean Sea, in the western parts of the Indian Ocean and the Pacific Ocean. The largest reef in the world is the Great Barrier Reef off north-eastern Australia. It is up to 72 kilometres (45 miles) wide and 2000 kilometres (1243 miles) long.

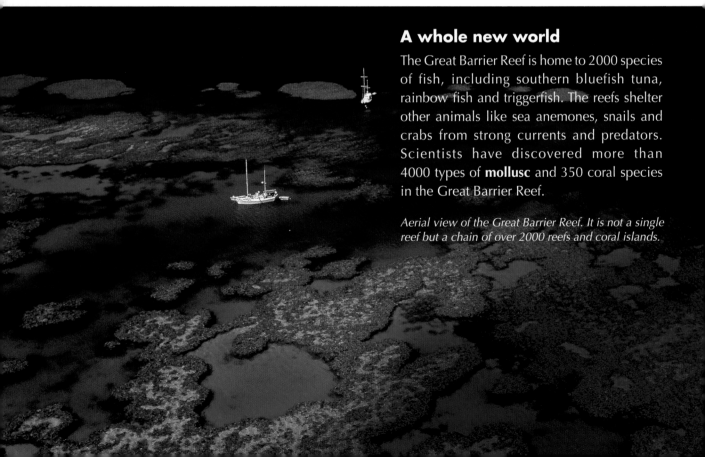

A whole new world

The Great Barrier Reef is home to 2000 species of fish, including southern bluefish tuna, rainbow fish and triggerfish. The reefs shelter other animals like sea anemones, snails and crabs from strong currents and predators. Scientists have discovered more than 4000 types of **mollusc** and 350 coral species in the Great Barrier Reef.

Aerial view of the Great Barrier Reef. It is not a single reef but a chain of over 2000 reefs and coral islands.

Bleached coral in the Great Barrier Reef.

The great bleaching event of 1998

Coral reefs have a skeleton made of calcium carbonate. This is a white, chalky material created by millions of tiny zooxanthellae, which are algae that live inside coral polyps. Zooxanthellae produce oxygen when they photosynthesize and this oxygen is used by the coral polyps. The zooxanthellae also add colour to the corals. When the temperature of the water rises above 29 °C (84.2 °F), they die. The corals lose their colouring and appear white. This phenomenon is known as coral bleaching.

There have been over 60 worldwide coral bleaching events since the 1980s. The year 1998 was the hottest in the 20th century. In the Great Barrier Reef, the sea temperature rose during the period January to March, reaching a peak of 32.7 °C (90.86 °F). As a result, up to 90 per cent of the corals there were bleached and 30 per cent were destroyed completely.

Will the corals recover?

Some of the corals do recover, but their **composition** may change. Scientists working on the Great Barrier Reef discovered that fast-growing corals like the staghorn coral do not recover as well as slow-growing species like the finger coral. Two years after the mass bleaching event in 1998, staghorn corals had grown by only 15 centimetres. This means that the new coral reef is likely to contain fewer staghorn corals than before.

Staghorn coral in the Great Barrier Reef. They provide protection for small fish.

More about corals

There are two kinds of coral: hard and soft. Hard corals have a hard skeleton. Examples of hard corals include the star, brain, finger and staghorn coral. Soft corals include sea fans, sea whips and sea rods. They move with the ocean currents. Both kinds of coral are anchored to the ocean floor. Some coral reefs take millions of years to grow. Corals like the staghorn coral grow up to 20 centimetres per year. Other corals, such as the star coral, may only grow 0.32 centimetres annually.

Plants and the warming planet

Global warming is bad news for plants. Strong winds can destroy trees and lightning storms may cause forest fires. A huge storm in 1994 blew across the Christmas Mountains in Canada, striking down approximately 30 million trees. Such storms could become more common as global warming continues.

Trees damaged in a hurricane.

Carbon dioxide fertilizer

Plants grow as a result of photosynthesis. The rate of photosynthesis is faster when temperatures are higher because there is more carbon dioxide in the atmosphere. Scientists have found that forests grow better in environments that are rich in carbon dioxide, at least for a while. This is known as the **fertilizing effect of carbon dioxide**. But there are other factors in the environment that plants need in order to grow. These include light, water and soil nutrients such as phosphorus and nitrogen. If these do not increase together with the increase in carbon dioxide levels, the trees will return to their normal growth pattern.

Plant migration

Global warming may cause some plant species to 'migrate'. Plants are very sensitive to the temperature of their environment. If their habitat becomes too warm, plants may die. The original **indigenous species** may be replaced by new **alien species** that thrive in the warmer environment. These new species will have migrated from their original habitat.

Scientists believe that some plants could migrate in the next 70 years by 300 to 400 kilometres (186 to 248 miles) towards the polar regions, or to altitudes 500 metres higher in order to find cooler habitats. About 10,000 years ago, as the climate warmed up following the last ice age, trees like birch, pine and oak began to spread across the UK, replacing the grasslands that had thrived there in the cooler and drier climate. But how did these species migrate there?

During the last ice age, much of the water in the oceans froze. Sea levels were lower than they are today. In Southeast Asia, they were up to 120 metres lower. Seas like the Straits of Malacca and the English Channel were dry. As a result, the seeds of trees and other plants were carried by animals and birds from the European continent across the English Channel.

Gnarled oak trees in Puzzle Wood, Dartmoor, UK.

Forest pests

Warmer climates may also bring an increase in harmful **pests**. The gypsy moth is one example. The moth caterpillar feeds on leaves of hardwood trees, such as oak and sugar maple, and can strip trees of their leaves very quickly. The eggs of the moth are destroyed by temperatures between –23 to –9 °C (–9.4 to 15.8 °F). The moth originally bred in Europe and Asia, but warmer winters mean that the gypsy moth can now live in areas that were previously too cold, such as Canada.

How do trees migrate?

Trees migrate by spreading their seeds. If a seed falls in a suitable environment, a new plant will grow. Different plant species have different rates of migration. The rate is related to the way plants spread their seeds and pollen. Very light seeds may be carried great distances on the wind, or by animals and birds. But seedlings will only grow if the new environment is suitable for them.

The Sundarbans

Mangrove forests are an important feature on the coasts of many tropical countries. The trees protect the coasts from strong waves. They also trap material carried by rivers as the water flows into the sea. This benefits the corals in the warm seas nearby as they need clear water to grow. Many fish, crabs and prawns produce their young in the forests, as the mangroves provide food and shelter from predators. The biggest threat to mangroves is rising sea levels. If the average sea level rises more than 1 metre, over 90 per cent of the existing mangrove trees in the world will drown.

The Sundarbans

The Sundarbans is the world's largest mangrove forest. It is located in the **delta** of the Ganges River along the coast of Bangladesh. It once covered an area of 182 square kilometres (70 square miles), but human activities such as deforestation and shrimp farming have destroyed much of the forest. In recent years, the sea levels have been rising steadily and submerging the mangrove trees. As a result, about 75 square kilometres (29 square miles) of the forest are now flooded.

Fishermen at work in the Sundarbans.

Flooded trees and dying mangroves

The flooded trees in the Sundarbans are dying. Mangrove plants grow in mud. The mud particles are so finely packed together that there is no oxygen in them. All plants need oxygen, so the mangrove plants raise their roots above the ground in order to breathe.

Some species, like the *Rhizophora*, breathe through stilt-like roots which grow above the ground. Others, like the *Avicennia*, have long, flat roots with pointed tips running parallel to the ground. When the mangroves are submerged, the *Avicennia* trees drown because their roots can no longer take in oxygen from the air.

Aerial roots of the Rizophora *help to anchor the plant in the soft mud. The roots also provide support for seedlings, which attach themselves to the parent plant. The seedlings drop off after a few weeks and begin to grow in the mud.*

Healthy trees in the Sundarbans mangrove forest.

Mangrove trees in a warmer climate

Mangroves growing on higher ground in the Sundarbans face another challenge. As the environment gets warmer, the trees lose water from their leaves more quickly and cannot grow well. Hotter weather may result in shorter trees with smaller leaves. Such trees are less healthy and more likely to become diseased. They are also more likely to be uprooted during storms.

Other uses of mangroves

If allowed to grow, these mangrove seedlings will continue to provide food and fuel for people. Mangroves are natural habitats for shellfish, crabs, lobsters and fish. Parts of the mangrove tree can also be used to make sunscreen, mosquito repellants and anti-cancer drugs.

Animals and the warming planet

Global warming can affect the life cycles of animals. When winters are shorter, birds lay their eggs earlier in spring. The North American tree swallow, for example, lays its eggs an average of nine days earlier than it did 40 years ago. Studies in Europe and North America also show that some migratory bird species are arriving at their destination about ten to twelve days earlier than before. These changes in timing could mean that there may not be a ready supply of the usual food sources for the nestlings that hatch earlier and for the migrating birds that arrive earlier. This lack of food could reduce their numbers.

Closer to the north

Scientists say that, on average, animal species are moving 6 kilometres (3.7 miles) closer to the North Pole every ten years. The sooty copper butterfly, which was originally found in Barcelona, Spain, migrated to Austria. More recently, over a period of just five years, it has been found in Estonia, even further north.

A sooty copper butterfly.

Where is the grass?

Global warming has resulted in increased rainfall in places like Siberia, Alaska and Scandinavia. Some parts are covered by ice and snow all year round. Rain water seeps into the snow and forms a layer of ice over the soil and any grass growing below the ice. Reindeer and elk cannot break this ice layer in order to eat the grass. As a result, 10,000 reindeer starved to death in Chukotsk Peninsula, Siberia, in 1996 and 1997.

Marine life – for better or worse?

The warming oceans also affect fish and other marine animals. Warmer temperatures increase the metabolic rate of Pacific salmon, which is the speed at which their bodies function. This means that the fish have to eat more food to survive in the warmer waters. In 1997 and 1998, fishermen found that the number of Pacific salmon in Alaska fell when the ocean temperature rose by 3 °C (5.4 °F). Some species, like the sockeye salmon, may soon face extinction.

*Left: Dead salmon **fry** in Alaska. Below: Scientists have found that a polar bear loses 10 kilograms for every week it does not hunt seals.*

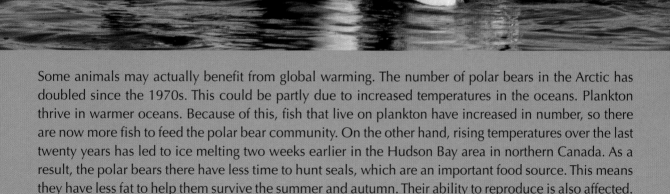

Some animals may actually benefit from global warming. The number of polar bears in the Arctic has doubled since the 1970s. This could be partly due to increased temperatures in the oceans. Plankton thrive in warmer oceans. Because of this, fish that live on plankton have increased in number, so there are now more fish to feed the polar bear community. On the other hand, rising temperatures over the last twenty years has led to ice melting two weeks earlier in the Hudson Bay area in northern Canada. As a result, the polar bears there have less time to hunt seals, which are an important food source. This means they have less fat to help them survive the summer and autumn. Their ability to reproduce is also affected.

Disease

Many of the bacteria and viruses that cause diseases such as malaria cannot survive in cold climates. Scientists think that global warming has allowed viruses and bacteria to thrive in places that were once too cold for them to survive. The heat also makes the **immune systems** of animals less effective, making it harder for them to fight off an illness. This may be why malaria is now found in birds that live in cold places like the Hawaiian mountains.

CASE STUDY

The Rocky Mountains

The Rocky Mountains, in the USA, stretch north to south for more than 4827 kilometres (3000 miles), from north-west Alaska to Mexico. The highest mountain, Mount Elbert, peaks at 4399 metres.

Animals of the Rocky Mountains

The Rocky Mountains are home to animals and birds like the bighorn sheep, the marmot, the white winter owl and the American robin. The American robin is the largest of the North American thrushes. It has a grey coat and a reddish underside. Once winter is over, American robins make an annual flight up the Rocky Mountains to lay their eggs.

Marmots look like squirrels. They live on plants that grow high up on the mountains. Marmots **hibernate** for eight months of each year. When winter is over, the animals sense the change in temperature. They wake from their hibernation and begin to look for food.

Waiting for the snow to melt

Scientists have found that over the last twenty years, spring has been arriving earlier in the lower parts of the Rocky Mountains. The snow on the lower slopes starts to melt fourteen days earlier than it does at the top. When the American robin arrives at the mountain top, it has to wait for another two weeks for the snow there to melt. Only then can it find food and start to make a nest. During that time, the robin faces the risk of starvation.

An American robin with its chicks. The female usually lays three or four eggs which take around two weeks to hatch. Adult robins may reach around 25 centimetres in length. Their food consists of fruit, insects and snails.

Mountain warming

If the Earth does warm up, the great snow-capped mountain peaks like the Rocky Mountains will warm up nearly three times faster than other regions. Snow and ice are shiny surfaces that reflect sunlight back into space. When they are gone, the darker-coloured ground and rock will absorb more heat. Scientists have found that while the average global temperature has increased by 0.6 °C (1 °F), the temperature on the Rocky Mountains has increased by 1.5 °C (2.7 °F). This is nearly three times the global average.

A marmot suns itself in Glacier National Park, Montana. Marmots are the largest members of the squirrel family. They build complex underground burrows.

Waking up earlier from hibernation

Scientists have also noticed that marmots are waking from hibernation an average of 38 days earlier than they did twenty years ago. But the snow high up on the mountains does not begin to melt until about two weeks after they wake. So, like the American robin, the marmots may not be able to find enough food. Having just emerged from a long sleep, they do not have the energy to move down the Rocky Mountains to the warmer parts where the snow has already melted. As a result, the marmots may starve to death.

Living on a warming planet

One-third of the world's people lives within 60 kilometres (37 miles) of a sea coast. In countries like the Netherlands and Bangladesh, more than half of the population lives near rivers or the coast.

Coastal dwellings in Bangladesh. The coastline of Bangladesh is 580 kilometres (361 miles) long.

Threat from the rising seas

Scientists think that the world's oceans could rise by 20 centimetres by 2050. These rising seas would flood low-lying islands. For example, the Maldives in the Indian Ocean is a nation made up of 1190 islands. Nearly all the islands are barely 2 metres above sea level. If sea levels rise more than this, the Maldives will disappear under water. States along the US coast are also in danger of being flooded. If sea levels were to increase by just 1.5 metres, Miami in the state of Florida would be completely covered with water.

Aerial view of the Maldives. Only about 200 of the 1190 islands are inhabited by people.

Spreading tropical diseases

Tropical diseases like dengue fever and malaria are transmitted by mosquitoes. The mosquitoes that carry such diseases live in warm places and cannot survive the cooler weather in temperate places like Europe or North America. However, as the weather gets warmer, mosquitoes will be able to survive and reproduce in places that were once too cold for them. In 2001, doctors reported more than 250 cases of malaria in New York.

The Aedes mosquito having a feast.

Growing food

Global warming will also affect crops. Plants are sensitive to changes in weather and soil conditions. A continuous warm spell in summer means that soils become drier. This is because the warmer weather melts any snow earlier and the land has a longer time to dry out. When it is near harvest time, the soil may not be moist enough for crops like corn and potatoes to grow properly. In 1998, over 90 per cent of the crops in Texas, USA, withered during a hot spell.

Corn withering in a drought in Tanzania.

Drought and diseases

A warming planet means that drought will occur more often. This will affect people's health. When rivers dry out, **microorganisms**, germs and bacteria in the water are concentrated in small puddles. Any disease-causing organisms in these puddles will pass into humans and animals drinking from the puddles. They are more likely to fall ill as a result. People get cholera, a disease that causes severe diarrhoea, by drinking unclean water. In 2002, medical workers reported over 350 cases of cholera in Zimbabwe. Doctors think that the outbreak was caused by the drought.

Florida, the Sunshine State

The state of Florida lies at the south-eastern tip of the USA and covers 170,300 square kilometres (65,753 square miles). To the south of the state is the Atlantic Ocean, which brings warm ocean breezes to its beaches. Every year, thousands of visitors flock to southern Florida to sunbathe on its beaches and see the wildlife in the Florida Everglades.

Global warming is a problem facing Florida. Over the last century, average temperatures in Florida have increased from 19.4 °C (67 °F) between 1892 and 1921 to over 20.5 °C (69 °F) between 1966 and 1995. Scientists project that average temperatures there will rise even further. As sea levels rise, sea water will advance inland and affect crops, buildings and the fragile ecosystems of the Florida Everglades.

Damage to coastal areas

Around 95 per cent of Florida's 14 million people live within 56 kilometres (35 miles) of the coast. If sea levels were to rise by about 1 metre, the water would move inland by as much as 122 metres in some places. This would flood beaches and damage houses and hotels built near the coast. Tourism in Florida would also be affected.

Hotels along Miami Beach, Florida.

Damage to crops

The growing of citrus fruits, such as oranges, grapefruit and tangerines, is the most important form of agriculture in Florida. Other crops include sugarcane, tomatoes and flowers. Together, these bring the USA about US$8 billion a year. A warmer climate will reduce the **yield** of all these crops. This is because rising sea levels will flood the cropland with sea water for at least part of the year. This flooding will damage plant roots and eventually kill them. Also, when sea water seeps into the ground, it leaves salt in the soil and crops cannot survive in salt-rich soil.

An orange grove in Florida.

The Florida Everglades is one of Florida's top tourist attractions. Although global warming is a serious problem, tourism and environmental damage are already destroying the fragile ecosystems of the Everglades.

Damage to ecosystems

Rising sea levels could also damage the unique ecosystems of the Florida Everglades and the Big Cypress Swamp, which together cover 6993 square kilometres (2700 square miles) of southern Florida. These are home to a wide variety of plants, animals and wading birds that come to nest there. The population of wading birds has already declined. Since the 1930s, the number of birds that nest there has fallen from around 265,000 to a low of 10,000 in the 1990s.

Less fresh water to drink

A rise in sea levels affects fresh water supplies. Most of Florida's fresh drinking water comes from underground sources. The swamps in southern Florida are drained by canals that extend to the sea. During times of drought, sea water flows inland along these canals. The sea water can then seep into the ground and contaminate the fresh water supply. Scientists say that sea water has already seeped into Miami's underground water supply. Higher temperatures also means an increase in the rate of evaporation, which could reduce water supplies, especially during hot summers.

World leaders meet

In June 1992, 108 world leaders from countries including the USA, the UK and Australia as well as delegates from 178 countries gathered in Rio de Janeiro, Brazil, to discuss environmental issues. These issues included climate change, pollution and forest protection. The conference is known as the United Nations Conference on Environment and Development (UNCED), and also the Earth Summit. It was an important event as it forced the leaders to discuss environmental issues at a high level.

World leaders at the Earth Summit.

UN Framework Convention on Climate Change

The world leaders held many meetings. In one meeting, known as the UN Framework Convention on Climate Change, some of the leaders agreed to reduce their countries' greenhouse gas emission levels. They aimed to do so by the year 2000, but this target was not met.

Children gather below the Tree of Life, a sculpture unveiled at the Earth Summit.

The birth of the Kyoto Protocol

The leaders met again in 1997 in Kyoto, Japan, to adjust their 1992 agreement on climate change. The new agreement to cut down greenhouse gas emissions was named the Kyoto **Protocol**. In the Kyoto Protocol, many leaders promised to reduce greenhouse gas emissions by 5 per cent of the amounts recorded in the 1990s. They also agreed to achieve this target by 2018. The Kyoto Protocol is expected to take effect by 2008.

Aerial view of New York City. The USA was one of the countries that signed the Protocol. In 2001, President George W Bush withdrew from the agreement when he came into office. This move angered many countries.

The International Children's Conference on the Environment

Every two years, the United Nations Environment Programme (UNEP) holds an International Children's Conference on the Environment for children between the ages of ten and thirteen. During the meeting, children learn about current environmental issues. They also share their views on topics such as deforestation and global warming. The first conference was held in 1995 in Eastbourne, UK. It lasted for three days, during which 800 participants from over 90 countries discussed recycling, environmental protection and endangered wildlife.

Tropical rainforest along the Congo River in Africa.

The World Summit

More recently, in 2002, world leaders held another conference in Johannesburg, South Africa. This conference is known as the World Summit. At this meeting, the USA pledged US$43 million to promote the efficient use of energy and another US$53 million to preserve the tropical rainforests in the Congo Basin in central Africa.

Fighting water

The Netherlands lies between Germany and Belgium on the north-west coast of Europe. It has a total land area of 41,526 square kilometres (16,033 square miles). This is almost twice the size of New Jersey, USA. The Netherlands means 'the low land' in the Dutch language. More than half of the country is made up of low-lying land facing the North Sea. Its average height is only 94 centimetres above sea level. About 60 per cent of the population of 16 million lives near the coast or beside rivers.

A traditional wind-powered pump for draining water from cropland. About 26 per cent of the land in the Netherlands is set aside for growing crops like fruits, potatoes and sugar beets. Today, modern pumps have replaced the traditional ones.

The threat from the ocean

Much of the Netherlands consists of land reclaimed from the sea over the past 800 years. This land has since been used for agriculture. The country faces a serious threat of flooding if sea levels rise as a result of global warming. Most of the coastal areas are lower than the present sea level. The lowest point in the country, Zuidplaspolder, is 7 metres below sea level. Scientists estimate that by 2050, parts of the country will sink by another 41 centimetres.

In the flood of 1953, the sea poured in and swept more than 64 kilometres (40 miles) inland.

The country has already experienced massive flooding in the past. In the North Sea Flood of 1953, strong winds and high tides raised the sea level around the coast by more than 3 metres. This disaster flooded nearly 2000 square kilometres (772 square miles) of land, killed about 2000 people and left almost 100,000 people homeless.

Stepping back

Global warming may bring drier summers and wetter winters to the Netherlands. Scientists warn that rainfall may be so abundant that riverbanks will burst and overflow. Instead of fighting the floods, the Dutch government plans to let the rivers overflow naturally. The authorities call this plan 'making space for water'. They plan to resettle the people who live on 900 square kilometres (348 square miles) of very low land by 2050. The authorities hope that forest and marshland will grow on this land. They also plan to convert 250 square kilometres (96.5 square miles) of land into areas where flood water can be stored in temporary pools.

Stopping the sea's advance

To protect the land from flooding, the Dutch government has built **dykes** and storm barriers. These are important because much of the land is reclaimed from the sea. Dykes along the coast and next to rivers help keep out sea water and river water. The system of dykes stretches about 400 kilometres (249 miles) and is strong enough to withstand water surging at the rate of 13,000 cubic metres per second. The authorities have also built special barriers to keep water out during severe storms. The New Waterway Barrier, built in 1997, is about 300 metres long and weighs more than 15,000 tonnes. According to engineers, this barrier can protect about 1 million people living inside and around the city of Rotterdam.

This huge dyke separates the North Sea and the Netherlands.

More about dykes

In some places, there are many dykes behind each other. These are called the 'watchers', 'sleepers' and 'dreamers'. The watchers are massive sea-walls facing the coast. The sleepers are smaller walls behind the watchers. The dreamers are thinner inland barriers around farms and homes.

Storing carbon

The term **carbon sequestration** describes how carbon dioxide can be stored naturally rather than allowing it to escape into the atmosphere. As carbon dioxide is a greenhouse gas, the more of it there is in the atmosphere, the warmer the planet will become. Planting trees is one way of sequestering carbon dioxide. As trees grow, they absorb carbon dioxide from the atmosphere and use it to make wood. All the plants in the world together can retain about 600 gigatonnes of carbon.

Protecting the forests of Western Australia

The Department of Conservation and Land Management (CALM) protects and **conserves** the environment, wildlife and natural resources in Western Australia. CALM cares for over 240,000 square kilometres (92,664 square miles) of land, in the form of nature reserves, wildlife parks, state forests and timber reserves.

Erskine Falls in the Angahook-Lorne State Park in Victoria, Australia.

Sharefarming in Western Australia

CALM set up a sharefarming project in the late 1980s, partly as a way of storing carbon dioxide. In this project, timber companies plant blue gum trees on farmland where farmers grow various crops. The trees provide shelter for the crops and for farm animals. The farmers charge the timber companies for the space taken up by the blue gum trees. Over 1200 square kilometres (463 square miles) of trees have been planted through this project. The timber companies plan to plant 6000 square kilometres (2316 square miles) of maritime pine over the next 30 years. In all, these trees could sequester as much as 180 megatonnes of carbon dioxide from the atmosphere.

Eucalyptus trees in Australia. The blue gum tree is related to the eucalyptus tree. Eucalyptus trees are grown to provide timber, gum and an oil that is used in medicines.

Working together

CALM has also worked with Australian industries and farmers to explore how new plantations can be set up. Oil companies British Petroleum (BP) and Chevron Australia Private Limited agreed in 1999 to plant 30 square kilometres (11.6 square miles) of trees. The Oil Mallee Association and Oil Mallee Company Oil plan to establish mallee plantations in Western Australia. These would be able to sequester more than 800 megatonnes of carbon dioxide over the next 40 years.

Fruit of a mallee tree. Mallee is related to the eucalyptus tree. The oil from its leaves is used to make vapour rubs.

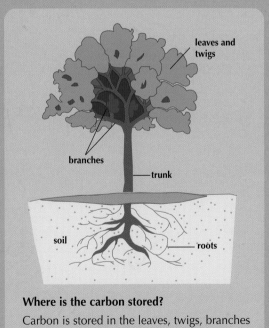

leaves and twigs

branches

trunk

soil

roots

Where is the carbon stored?
Carbon is stored in the leaves, twigs, branches and trunk of a plant. Carbon is also stored in the soil.

New methods, new devices

Scientists are now inventing new devices that use less fossil fuels or give off fewer greenhouse gases. These include energy-saving light bulbs that use less electricity but are just as bright as normal bulbs and cars that use less petrol. One such car, which uses both electricity and petrol at the same time, will be tested in the near future.

These houses in the Netherlands are fitted with solar panels. The panels absorb the heat from the Sun to provide warmth in winter.

The Climate Trust

The Climate Trust is a non-profit organization that provides money for projects that reduce carbon dioxide emissions. This organization, originally known as the Oregon Climate Trust, was formed in 1997. In that year, the Oregon state authorities needed to find ways of absorbing about 17 per cent of their carbon dioxide emissions. They paid the Climate Trust to help them, and the Trust used the money to support projects that reduce or sequester carbon dioxide emissions. In all, the projects supported by the Climate Trust will absorb about 844,000 tonnes of atmospheric carbon dioxide over the next 10 to 100 years.

A landfill site. Landfills release carbon dioxide and methane, which contribute to global warming.

Recycling methane

Some companies collect methane from landfill sites to use as fuel. One example is Tucson Electric Power, an electrical company in Arizona, the USA. It collects methane from the Los Reales landfill site in Tucson and burns it instead of coal to produce electricity. Other countries, such as the UK, Canada and Egypt, are also recovering methane from landfill sites.

Environmentally-friendly fuel cells

Scientists are finding ways to use fuel cells to power cars and heat and light houses. These cells combine oxygen and hydrogen gas to produce electricity. The wonderful thing about fuel cells is that they produce water instead of carbon dioxide. Some international companies, such as the United Technologies Corporation, have already made different types of fuel cells to run cars and home appliances.

A three-wheeled, solar-powered, electric car parked at Gstaad, Switzerland.

In a nutshell

Global warming:

- causes drought
- destroys crops
- damages ecosystems
- upsets the natural life cycles of plants and animals
- brings about more violent storms and severe flooding to lowland areas
- makes the Earth a hotter place to live in.

What can I do?

Help conserve our environment! We can all do our part to reduce the amount of greenhouse gases in the atmosphere and protect the Earth from global warming. Here are some ways you can help.

Play your part at home

- Stop junk mail coming into your home. Write to Mailing Preference Service, DMA House, 70 Margaret Street, London W1W 8SS, and tell them that you do not wish to receive such mail. This will reduce your family's junk mail by up to 75 per cent, saving up to 1.5 trees per person per year.

- Use rechargeable batteries to power electronic items. This reduces the number of batteries you throw away and in turn reduces the amount of waste that is burned at incinerators.

- Ask your parents to set the temperature of your hot water heater to 54 °C (130 °F), so electricity or natural gas is not used up unnecessarily.

- Ask your parents to replace normal light bulbs with energy-efficient flourescent bulbs wherever possible. On a large scale, it means fewer fossil fuels are burned and global warming will slow down.

- Wash clothes or dishes only when there is a full load. Turn off the hot air drying function on your dishwasher.

- If it is not possible to do any of the above, then switching off lights or fans every time you leave a room will help, too.

Children gather used plastic bottles for recycling.

Women are employed to clean used plastic bags at a polythene-recycling factory in Bangladesh. In developed countries, large supermarket chains give away 300 million plastic shopping bags a year. The lifespan of a plastic bag is about 400 years. This means that more landfill sites have to be created to dispose of these bags. Plastics can be burned, but the burning releases toxic gases into the atmosphere.

Get involved

- Join an organization that works to reduce waste and protect the environment, such as Kids For a Clean Environment (http://www.kidsface.org).

Shop smart

- When you are shopping, buy products with a 'Recyclable' sign *(left)* on them. Recyclable products are usually made from recycled materials. These products also need less energy to make, so less fuel is burned in the manufacturing process.
- Look for products that are environmentally friendly. These products have a mark to say that they have been certified. The Greenhouse Friendly mark used in Australia is an example. It means that the Australian Greenhouse Office has certified that these products do not release harmful greenhouse gases into the environment.
- Instead of using plastic bags to bring your purchases home, use canvas bags or baskets. These are durable, washable and reusable.

See the greenhouse effect at work

Try this experiment to see the effects of greenhouse gases. You will need two alcohol thermometers, two glass jars, a can of fizzy soft drink, water, sticky tape and clingfilm.

- Tape a thermometer inside each jar. Make sure that the bulb of the thermometer is 6 centimetres above the bottom of each jar.
- Pour the fizzy drink into one jar and water into the other jar to a level of 3 centimetres.
- Cover both jars with clingfilm and leave them for one hour.
- When the hour is up, read the temperature on each of the thermometers.

What do you notice about the temperature reading on the thermometers in both jars? You will see that the temperature in the jar of carbonated drink is higher. Carbonated drinks release bubbles of carbon dioxide gas as they fizz. The carbon dioxide enters the air in the jar and is trapped by the clingfilm. Carbon dioxide is a greenhouse gas. It traps heat in the air, so the temperature rises.

Glossary

alien species plant or animal that moves from its original habitat into a new area

asphalt brownish-black solid substance used to pave roads and build roofs

atom smallest particle of a substance

bacteria microscopic organisms that have one cell and can cause disease

carbon sequestration storing of carbon in natural sources so that it does not enter the atmosphere

composition mixture of parts that form a whole

conserve protect from harm and prevent wasteful use of resources

cross-section section formed when an object is sliced in half

decomposition process in which organic matter is broken down

deforestation removal of forest. Forests may be removed as a source of timber, to clear the land for farms or cities, or by natural processes.

delta area of low, flat land where a river splits and spreads out into several branches before entering the sea

dyke thick wall that is built to stop water flooding on to very low-lying land from a river or sea

ecosystem community of plants and animals within a physical environment

fertilizing effect of carbon dioxide phenomenon in which increased carbon dioxide causes plants to grow bigger and faster

fossil fuel fuel derived from the fossilized remains of plants and animals. Examples of fossil fuels are coal and petroleum.

fry small, young fish

geological relating to geology, which is the study of the Earth's structure, surface and origins

gigatonne unit of measurement. One gigatonne is equal to 1 thousand million tonnes.

glacier large body of ice that moves very slowly

greenhouse effect phenomenon in which gases in the Earth's atmosphere trap heat

greenhouse gas gas that traps heat in the Earth's atmosphere

habitat natural environment of an animal or plant where it lives and grows

heat wave period of unusually hot weather

hemisphere one of the halves of the Earth that lie on either side of the equator

hibernate spend the winter in a deep sleep-like state

humidity amount of moisture in the air

immune system series of reactions in the body which protects it from disease. When disease-causing germs enter the body, the immune system releases antibodies that help fight them.

indigenous species plant or animal that is living in its original habitat

Industrial Revolution period between the 1700s and the 1800s when power-driven machinery began to replace human-powered tools

mathematician person who specializes in the study of numbers and calculations

megatonne unit of measurement. One megatonne is equal to 1 million tonnes.

meteorologist person who specializes in the study of the weather

migrate move from one habitat to another

microorganism very small living thing which can only be seen under a microscope

model miniature representation of something

mollusc marine animal that has a protective shell but no spine. Examples of molluscs are shellfish and snails.

ozone gas that consists of three atoms of oxygen

pest animal or plant that causes harm to other animals or plants

petroleum thick mixture of substances containing hydrogen and carbon. Petroleum occurs naturally under the Earth's surface.

photosynthesis process in which green plants make food in sunlight using carbon dioxide, water and sunlight

plankton microscopic organisms that float near the surface of lakes, rivers and oceans. Fish and other marine animals depend on plankton for food.

pollutant substance that contaminates

prehistoric relating to the time before people started recording historical events

pollen powdery yellow substance that plants produce as a way of making seeds and so creating new plants

protocol written record of an agreement made by two or more countries

radiate emit, or send, out rays or waves of energy

respire use oxygen to burn food to release energy

savanna flat grassland usually found near the tropics

soluble able to dissolve in water

ultraviolet (UV) invisible light rays in sunlight that can destroy skin cells and cause skin cancer

waterlogged soaked with water

yield amount of food produced on an area of land

Finding out more

Books:

Just the Facts: Global Population, Paul Brown
(Heinemann Library, 2002)

Taking Action: Friends of the Earth, Louise Spilsbury
(Heinemann Library, 2000)

Taking Action: World Wide Fund for Nature,
Louise Spilsbury (Heinemann Library, 2000)

World's Worst Fire Disasters, Rob Alcraft
(Heinemann Library, 1999)

Videos:

Earth at Risk – Global Warming, Schlessinger Media
(1993)

Global Warming: "Hot Enough For You?", News
Matters Series (2000)

The Sizzling Planet, The History Channel (1999)

Websites:

Atmospheric Radiation Measurement (ARM) Program
http://www.arm.gov/docs/education/globwarm/
globegin.html

Climate Action Network
http://www.climatenetwork.org

Earth Observatory
http://earthobservatory.nasa.gov

Eco-Portal – The Environmental Sustainability
Information Source
http://www.eco-portal.com/climate/information/
For_Kids

Environmental Protection Agency
http://www.epa.gov/globalwarming/kids

Greenpeace
http://archive.greenpeace.org/climate/climatefaq.html

World Almanac for Kids Online
http://www.worldalmanacforkids.com/explore/
environment3.html

Organizations:

Environmental Protection Agency (EPA)
Headquarters
Ariel Rios Building
1200 Pennsylvania Avenue, N.W.
Washington, DC 20460, USA
http://www.epa.gov/air/oaqps/index.html

The Climate Trust
516 SE Morrison Street, Suite 300
Portland, Oregon 97214 2343, USA
http://www.climatetrust.org

Climate Action Network Australia
Solarch Building
1408 Anzac Parade
Little Bay, NSW 2036, Australia
Phone: 0407 2276633
http:www.cana.net.au

Sierra Club
Headquarters
85 Second Street, 2nd Floor
San Francisco, CA 94105, USA
Phone: 415 977 5500 Fax: 415 977 5799
http://www.sierraclub.org

National Society for Clean Air and Environmental
Protection (NSCA)
44 Grand Parade
Brighton, BN2 9QA, UK
Phone: 01273 878770 Fax: 01273 606626
http://www.nsca.org.uk

Disclaimer: All the Internet addresses (URLs) given
in this book were valid at the time of going to press.
However, due to the dynamic nature of the Internet,
some addresses may have changed or sites may have
changed or ceased to exist since publication. While the
author and Publisher regret any inconvenience this may
cause readers, no responsibility for any such changes
can be accepted by either the author or the Publisher.

Index

atmosphere 4–5, 10–16, 18, 20, 24, 40
Antartica 6, 8
Arctic 6, 29
Australia 40
    blue gum tree 41
    Department of Conservation and Land Management 41
    oil mallee 41
    sharefarming 41

bacteria 14, 17, 19, 29
bracket fungi 13
Brazil 18

cattle 12, 14, 19, 21
calcium carbonate 13, 23
carbon 13, 18–19
carbon cycle 12-13, 41
carbon sequestration 40
carbon sinks 13, 17
charcoal 9
chlorophyll 12–13
Christmas Mountains 24
cities
    Atlanta 8
    Barcelona 28
    Kyoto 37
    London 21
    Miami 32, 35
    New York 33, 37
    Rio de Janeiro 36
    Taipei 20
    Vostok 8
Climate Trust 42
coal 19
coral 22–23, 26
    coral bleaching 23
    coral reef 21–22
    staghorn coral 23

Death Valley 8
decomposition 12–13, 18
deforestation 12, 18

Earth Summit 36
English Channel 25

fertilizing effect of carbon dioxide 24
fossil fuels 7, 9, 19, 42

Florida 34–35
    Big Cypress Swamp 35
    Florida Everglades 34–35
fungi 13
fuel cells 43

Ganges River 26
greenhouse effect 5–6, 16
Geological Time Scale 7
glaciers 20–21
global warming 7, 20, 24, 28–29, 38–39
Great Barrier Reef 22–23
greenhouse gas 5, 7, 14–16, 19, 21, 42
    carbon dioxide 4–5, 7, 9–10, 12–19, 24, 40–43
    methane 4–5, 14–17, 19, 43
    nitrous oxide 14–15, 17, 19
    ozone 4–5, 14–15
Guy Stewart Callendar 10
gypsy moth 25

Hurricane Floyd 20
Humphry Davy 15
Holocene 6–7
helium 11

ice ages 6, 25
ice caps 4, 20–21
Industrial Revolution 7, 9
interstadials 6
International Children's Conference on the Environment 37

Jean Baptiste Fourier 5
John Tyndall 5

Kyoto Protocol 37

lightning 17

Maldives 32
mangrove 26–27
    Avicennia 27
    Rhizophora 27
Mauna Kea 10
mollusc 22

nitrogen 5
natural gas 19

Netherlands 32, 38–39, 42
    North Sea Flood 38–39
    Zuidplaspolder 39
North American tree swallow 28

oxygen 5, 17, 23

petroleum 19
photosynthesis 12, 16, 23–24
plants
    birch 25
    eucalyptus 41
    oak 25
    pine 11, 25, 41
    maple 25
plankton 16, 29
polar bears 29
pollen 11

Quaternary Period 6, 7

rice 19
Rocky Mountains 30–31
    American robin 30–31
    bighorn sheep 30
    marmot 30–31

satellites 10
sooty copper butterfly 21, 28
Straits of Malacca 25
stratosphere 15
Sundarbans 26–27
Svante Arrhennius 5

termites 17–19
tree rings 9, 11

ultraviolet rays 15
United Nations Conference on Environment and Development 36
United Nations Framework on Climate Change 36
urban heat island effect 8

Venus 5

water vapour 5, 14
weather balloons 11
World Summit 37

zooxanthellae 23